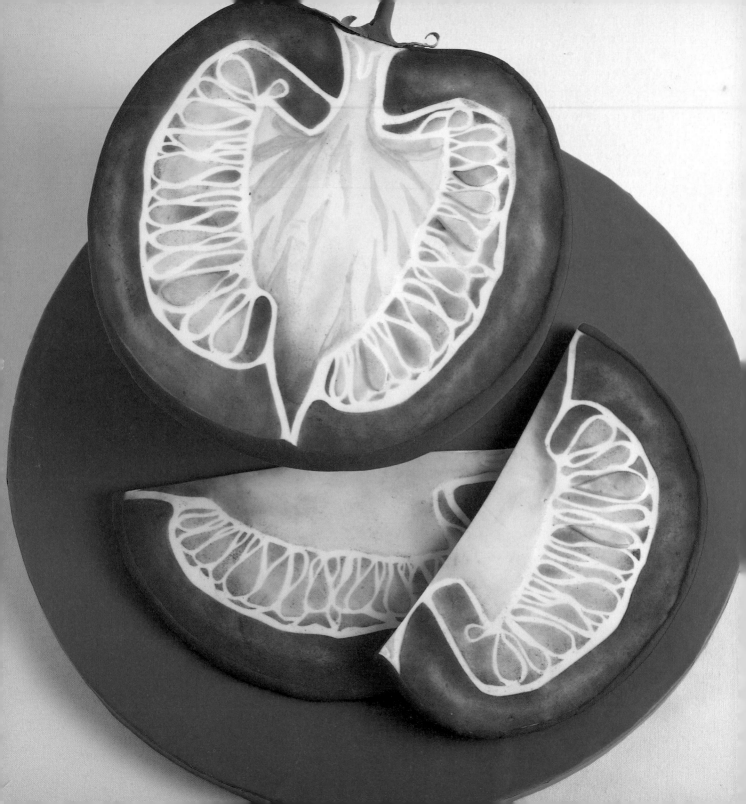

Letts Guides to Sugarcraft

Stencilling

AND 3-D WORK

SARAH GLEAVE

CONSULTANT: NICHOLAS LODGE

CHARLES LETTS
Letts
FOUNDED 1796

Designed and edited by
Anness Publishing Ltd
4a The Old Forge
7 Caledonian Road
London N1 9DX

First published 1991
by Charles Letts & Co Ltd
Diary House, Borough Road
London SE1 1DW

British Library Cataloguing in Publication
Data
Gleave, Sarah
    Stencilling and 3-D work.
    1. Cakes. Cookery
    I. Title
    641.8653

ISBN 1-85238–136–1

'Letts' is a registered trademark of
Charles Letts (Scotland) Ltd.

Editorial Director: Joanna Lorenz
Designer: Mike Snell
Photographer: Sue Atkinson

Printed and bound in Italy

To John, Kenzie, and Jessica.

I would like to thank Nick Lodge for his editorial consultancy;
Bronia, Alan, Sandra and Emma for being continuously on call in
times of need; and my family and friends for their valuable
contributions and support.

Original designs for the Christmas, Teddy and Clown cakes were
provided by Heather Snook of Ipswich, Suffolk.

Sarah Gleave offers courses in cake stencilling, and welcomes
enquiries addressed to Easter Poldar Farm, Kippen, Nr. Stirling,
Scotland.

Contents

Foreword

This book, *Stencilling and 3-D Work*, is one of three original books in a new series of guides to sugarcraft. Along with *Floral Sprays* and *Cake Styling*, it launches sugarcraft into new and exciting areas that have not been covered practically and visually in previous publications.

I first met Sarah two years ago when I stayed with her and her family while I was doing demonstrations and teaching classes in her area: she showed me some of her work, which was so refreshingly original and different from any other forms of stencilling that I had seen before that I told her she should write a book to share her talent with others.

The book is very easy to follow with step-by-step photographs and clear practical text, as well as gorgeous images of the finished cakes to inspire you. Careful use of colours is very important, but as Sarah states in her introduction only basic equipment is needed, and excellent results can be achieved even if you are attempting this fascinating aspect of sugarcraft for the first time.

I hope you will enjoy making some of the wonderful cakes in this book and will soon take things a step further when designing your own stencils and cakes; I would also like to congratulate Sarah on beautiful and creative work that I feel sure will be an inspiration to all of you.

Nicholas Lodge

Introduction

The popularity of stencilling as a technique and art has increased dramatically over recent years. Stencilled walls, furniture and fabrics are now a feature of many homes. I first began to explore the various uses and applications of stencilling when I was a ceramics student at Middlesex Polytechnic, as they are so quick to make and easy to use, and lead to such stunningly effective and stylish results.

I had always enjoyed cake designing and decorating for friends and relatives, like many other people, but I then began to experiment with stencils, taking the techniques I had learned elsewhere a step further and applying them to sugarpaste.

Stencilling is an ideal cake decorating technique, equally rewarding for those just beginning, when it can be used in a very simple way, and for those who would like to be a little more adventurous with their own ideas and designs. Experimenting with various images to produce original cakes is endlessly enjoyable and exciting, and has led to some highly imaginative creations that I believe are quite unique. The art of stencilling is by no means a new concept in cake decoration – it is the manner in which it is employed that is important. In this book I try to illustrate how a simple technique can develop many unusual characteristics. I have aimed to retain its simplicity and charm, yet at the same time introduce a fresh approach to its design.

Stencilling can be adapted to almost any theme or occasion, and I have included a wide variety of ideas and styles in order to show its versatility. There is a realistic tomato novelty cake, a three-tier wedding cake stylishly decorated with layers of freesias, simple ceramic tile-like plaque and panel features, and complex arrangements of free-standing flowers and three-dimensional butterflies.

Clear step-by-step photographs in full colour provide easy-to-follow instructions, inspiration and encouragement. The first part of the book gives basic information on the equipment required, and the essential techniques for creating your stencil. The materials required are inexpensive, and the techniques are straightforward and easy to master after a little practice. Stencilling is a quick and convenient form of decoration once the stencil has been cut, and providing it is washed and stored correctly it can be used again and again.

The main chapters demonstrate various ways of using stencils, some incorporating other sugarcraft techniques but all with the emphasis on stencilling. The projects range from those requiring only very basic artistic skills, to more intermediate patterns and then to quite advanced cake designs. Once you have mastered the techniques, you are well on the way to producing your own unique designs and creative stencilling masterpieces!

Sarah Gleave

BASIC EQUIPMENT

This is relatively inexpensive, and standard cake decorating tools and materials are all that are mainly required. Here is a basic check list of recommended items, available from most craft or artists' shops and cake decorating suppliers. The only special items you need for making stencils are a craft or x-acto knife, acetate and a cutting mat. Equipment like tilt boards isn't exactly essential, but I do find it can make your job very much easier, particularly when working on the sides of a cake. Revolving cake stands are also a useful investment if you do a lot of cake-making. Cake decorating colours – in paste or powder form – can be bought from many outlets; a few suppliers are listed on page 88.

1. Work surface – melamine, non-stick plastic, marble or ground glass.
2. Non-stick rolling pin.
3. Palette knife.
4. Cutting mat – this is worth buying as it makes light work of cutting a stencil and reduces the amount of blades you use.
5. Thick acetate or oiled parchment – available from any art or craft suppliers.
6. Black china marker or waterproof pen.
7. Craft knife for cutting out your stencils, and plenty of spare blades.
8. Paintbrushes – you will need a range of soft brushes. I have found that synthetic-haired brushes are more suitable for dusting as they hold the colour well.
9. Tilt board.

BASIC ICING RECIPES

These recipes have been used for all the cakes in this book. I generally use rolled fondant (sugarpaste) for the cake coverings with mexican and flower (gum) paste for stencilling and flower-work respectively. Mixed rolled fondant and gum tragacanth can be used for stencilled work, but does not guarantee such a quick or perfect result.

MEXICAN PASTE

Mexican paste is generally known for its use in figure modelling and bas-relief work. After experimentation, I found that it had the right qualities for stencilling: it is a very dense paste that stretches well without tearing too easily, which is particularly

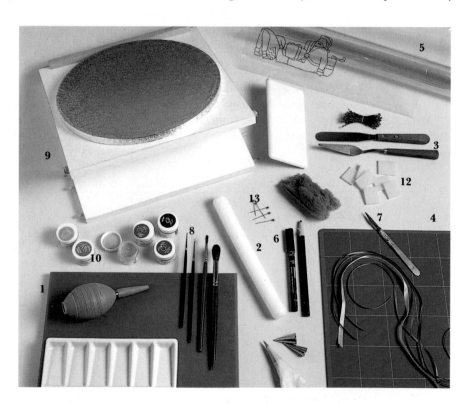

10. Edible dusting and paint colours.
11. Cornflour (cornstarch).
12. White fat.
13. Glass-headed pins.
14. Card.

useful when applying a stencilled design as a side decoration. It also has a very smooth texture and becomes very pliable when white fat is kneaded into it. This is ideal for rolling into a stencil. Finally, it dries very quickly, enabling the stencilled sections to be mounted onto the cake in some unusual ways.

INGREDIENTS:
225 g (8 oz/2 cups) icing
(confectioner's) sugar, sifted
15 ml (1 level tbsp) gum tragacanth
5 ml (1 tsp) liquid glucose
30 ml (6 tsp) cold water
rolled fondant (sugarpaste) or pastello

Sift the icing sugar and gum tragacanth onto a clean work surface. Make a well in the centre and add the liquid glucose. Add 5 teaspoons of the cold water – only add the 6th if the mixture is too firm. Begin mixing the paste, taking the sugar from the outside. Knead until all the ingredients are well blended together.

Weigh out an equal amount of rolled fondant (sugarpaste) or pastello and knead into the mexican paste.

Divide into 3 or 4 bags and store in an airtight container in the fridge until required. This paste will keep for approximately 2 to 3 months.

FLOWER PASTE
I use this paste for modelling flowers and butterflies. Alternatively, you can buy rolled fondant (sugarpaste) from any sugarcraft supplier and just add gum tragacanth.

INGREDIENTS:
425 g (14 oz/3.5 cups) icing (confectioner's) sugar, sifted
60 g (2 oz/0.5 cup) cornflour (cornstarch)
15 ml (1 tbsp) gum tragacanth or 10 ml (2 level tsp) gum tragacanth and 10 ml (2 tsp) carboxymethyl cellulose
25 ml (5 tsp) cold water
10 ml (2 tsp) powered gelatine
15 ml (1 tbsp) white fat (shortening)
10 ml (2 tsp) liquid glucose
white of 1 large egg, string removed

Sift together the icing sugar and cornflour in the bowl of a heavy mixer. Sprinkle on the gum tragacanth or gum tragacanth and carboxymethyl cellulose. Warm the mixer bowl over a large pan of boiling water and cover with a dry cloth and cakeboard. Leave for 10–15 minutes while you prepare the other ingredients.

Put the cold water in a small heatproof glass or cup, sprinkle on the gelatine and leave to sponge. Half fill a small saucepan with water and place over a low heat. Gently bring to just below boiling point, then place in the water the glass of gelatine, the container of liquid glucose and the beater of the mixer. When the gelatine appears clear, remove it from the pan and stir in the liquid glucose and white fat until the fat is melted.

When the icing sugar has been warmed, take the bowl off the pan of boiling water, dry the base and put onto the mixer. Remove and dry the beater from the other pan and attach. Pour in the gelatine solution and add the egg white. Cover the bowl with a cloth and turn the mixer onto its slowest speed. Once the ingredients are combined, turn the mixer to maximum and beat until the paste is white and stringy. This will take approximately 5–10 minutes.

Remove the paste from the bowl and divide into 4 or 5 clean plastic bags. Keep in an airtight container and refrigerate for at least 24 hours before using. To use the paste, cut off a small piece and knead in a little white fat and a tiny amount of egg white. The paste will soon become workable from the warmth of your hands.

ROYAL ICING
I always use powdered albumen for royal icing, as it is so quick and convenient. This is only suitable for basic work; when making fine lace work and runouts, pure 100% albumen is more suitable as it is stronger than artificial albumen.

INGREDIENTS:
15 ml (1 tbsp) albumen powder
75 ml (3 fl oz/0.4 cup) cold water
450 g (1 lb/4 cups) icing (confectioner's) sugar, sifted

Dissolve the albumen in the cold water and leave to stand for about 30 minutes, stirring occasionally. Put the sugar in the bowl of an electric mixer and pour in the albumen. Mix, using the beater, for about 12–15 minutes until it reaches a soft piping consistency.

MAKING AND USING STENCILS

I make my own individually-designed acetate stencils for all my cakes, which involves drawing up an original design, copying it onto acetate with a waterproof pen, then cutting the shape out of the acetate with a sharp craft knife. (The cut-out area on the stencil is what the finished picture will be.) Details are given here on how to adapt the designs in this book to the size required for your cake, and how to make them into stencils.

Some pre-cut commercial stencils are also available, although designs are limited and if they are made from stainless steel they would not be suitable for sugarcraft work.

Using the Designs in this Book

Designs for all the cakes in this book have been provided. You will probably need to alter them to fit them to the size of cake you wish to decorate; the amount they need to be enlarged to fit the specific cake in the photograph is different for each. To enlarge a drawing, you can either go to a photocopying or print shop and have a copy blown up (or reduced) to your specifications, or you can copy out the original design to a different size using the grid method. Once you have a drawing of the size required, it can be traced onto acetate as described opposite.

It is also important to note when drawing up and cutting your design that the bridge-like links, which hold the stencil together, should occur at regular intervals. If they do not, the whole structure will be extremely delicate to handle. For example, for the design on the Christening cake (page 24), I had to incorporate a regular diagonal slant on the hoop. Generally, wherever there is a line breaking up areas of colour, a thin bridge should be cut. Sometimes, on a very complicated design, it will not be

The Grid Method

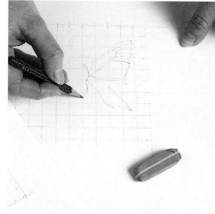

1 First trace the required image onto tracing paper.

2 Draw a neat square around the image, fitting tightly around the outside edge. Divide each side into 10 equal parts, and join the lines up from top to bottom and side to side to make a grid.

3 Now draw a square, of the size you want the finished stencil to be, on another piece of paper. Fill with grid lines as above. Then, copy the design from the smaller square to the larger, following the lines within each tiny box as a guide to where your pencil should go.

possible to cut bridges for every detail, so just choose the main features and cut bridges between those – quite simple divisions of colour on a stencil can still be very effective. The more practice you have, the greater your skill in cutting intricate stencils will become!

Beware when working on a dense and complicated design as much of its main body will be cut away, making it very weak. The width of the bridges should vary according to the size of the stencil, i.e. the smaller the design, the smaller the bridges should be. It is sometimes worth blocking out in advance with solid colour the areas that are to be cut away, so that mistakes when cutting can be avoided.

Making up Designs from other Images

You can also use the grid method to make up a design of your choice from any image, such as from a book or card (see pages 11–12 for ideas). However, once you have the image, it may be too complicated or detailed to be suitable for stencilling. So, once you have traced your drawing it can be simplified from a detailed image into a basic block design. You will need to work on the drawing so that it can be easily cut out as a flat pattern.

Transferring the Design onto Acetate

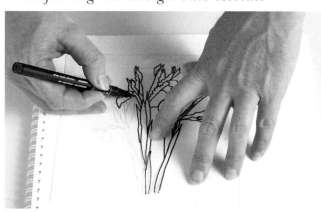

Cutting the Stencil

Acetate or oiled parchment can be used to make your stencil. I prefer to use acetate as it has several advantages: the design can be traced directly from your original image onto acetate, as it is transparent; the drawing is clearly defined; the stencil can be easily cleaned for re-use.

Cut a piece of acetate approximately 2 cm (¾″) larger than your drawing. Place the drawing underneath and trace the design onto the acetate, using a black china marker or waterproof pen. If you are using oil parchment, first trace the design onto tracing paper and then transfer it to the parchment with a soft HB pencil. Make sure that you keep a master copy of your original design; if you find that after continuous use your stencil is no longer as crisp, you will have a detailed drawing from which to reproduce your design.

Place the stencil design on a cutting mat and cut out using a sharp craft knife. Take time and care at this stage. It is worth doing a neat job to ensure a crisp and clean edge to your stencil. The knife has a tendency to slip across the acetate so make sure you apply firm pressure.

If you do make mistakes, such as cutting across your bridge work, acetate can be repaired with sticky tape and parchment with masking tape. This is done by simply pressing a piece of tape on the back of the damaged area and re-cutting on the right side. However, such mistakes may be detected on your finished piece of work, so try to avoid making errors. This will come with practice!

Finally, wash your stencil with warm soapy water and a soft brush on a flat surface, rinse and dry flat. Do not immerse in hot water as it may warp and be ruined.

Preparing the Stencil for Dusting

This is probably the most enjoyable aspect of making your stencil. Before you begin, lay out the colours and brushes that you will require. Take a small piece of prepared mexican paste (see page 6) and knead in some white fat to make it pliable and slightly moist. This will help to stick the paste onto the stencil.

1 Roll out the paste approximately 2 mm (1/16") thick on a non-stick board, large enough to cover the complete area of the design. Lift the paste off carefully onto a rolling pin and lay the stencil on the board face down.

2 Quickly roll the paste directly over the top of the stencil and gently rub across the surface with your fingertips, until you can see a slight impression of the image through the back. Avoid having any creases.

3 Immediately, place another board on top, lift everything up together and turn over. Remove the non-stick board, making sure the stencil does not peel off at the same time. Speed is the essence of success.

4 This iris is a good example to show the colouring process, as it has contrasting pale and dark shades to work on. The colour is applied to the paste, initially with a 'pouncing' brush action. Using direct brush strokes would be too unsubtle.

Mix the yellow with a little cornflour (cornstarch) and gently pounce the colour across the surface. Now change your brush and begin working on the blue areas. Use the same pouncing technique but gradually fade the blue into the yellow. Then brush over the tips of each petal in a darker mixture of mauve and blue. Clean or change your brush once again, and complete the rest of the design in various shades of green.

5 When you are quite sure that all areas have been covered, remove the excess dust using a puffer. Carefully peel off the acetate stencil. Trim around the edge of the plaque and allow to dry thoroughly. If possible, transfer to a porous surface at this stage to speed up the drying process.

Finish off the stencil by painting on the finer details such as the petals and leaves. This is done with a mixture of paste colour and clear alcohol. The plaque is now complete and can be placed on top of a cake as a simple form of stencil decoration. Many stencil designs in this book can be used simply in this way if you prefer. Also, once the cake has been cut, the plaque can be taken off and framed as an extra gift.

Care of the Stencils

Once you have used your stencil pattern make sure that it is cleaned thoroughly. Brush it with warm soapy water, rinse under cold or lukewarm running water and dry on tissue paper or kitchen roll before storing flat ready for further use. This is important, as carelessness could ruin the chances of re-using a stencil which may have taken several hours to draw up and cut out. If you intend to keep several stencils together, place thin sheets of paper in between each pattern to prevent them catching one another.

SOURCES OF IMAGERY

Inspiration and visual appeal are very personal things. Sources of imagery can be both primary and secondary: primary being drawn by you from nature itself and man-made objects, and secondary being drawn from ready-drawn and published images. If you consider the variety of ways in which cakes have been decorated in the past, you will be aware of the many themes and images that are used repeatedly.

Flowers probably have the widest appeal as there is always a favourite for everyone, from a simple buttercup or freesia to a highly cultivated rose. They have been depicted in just about every form you can think of – piped, modelled, painted, embroidered. Of course it is the way in which the image is perceived and interpreted that is important. Birds, butterflies and landscapes are other popular sources of imagery that are easily adapted to make many pictures and patterns. Look around and you will find many of these themes in textiles, jewellery and furniture. A simple design drawn from a detail of such imagery can be repeated to provide decorative borders for collar work or a frieze effect. If you have the time, it is worth making sketches of items that please you, such as flowers that are in bloom, even if you don't intend to use them immediately: at least they will be there to work from and inspire you at a later date.

Secondary sources include greeting cards, books, photographs, etc. Many well-known fictional characters can be easily adapted into simple drawings, suitable to work from in order to make a stencil pattern. I have accumulated a scrapbook of cards, tearsheets, photographs, etc. to use as a source of inspiration, and a variety of attractive borders and geometric patterns – details of which, in a simple arrangement, can produce some most effective and intricate designs. For the stencil creator, inspiring sources of imagery are endless.

USING FOOD COLOURS

Cake specialists sell a wide range of food colours in liquid, paste and powder form. There is also a wide variety of lustre colours on the market. Of course, the range of colours you can use is not confined to those you can buy. Mixing two or more shades together will create further colours. I also often blend cornflour (cornstarch) into the dusting colours to make them more subtle and to help provide a more even application onto the icing.

Colour control is a very important aspect of stencilling, and the key to a good result. Controlling the density and fading the colours in and out takes a little practice. It is worth experimenting so that you begin to get a feel of how they should be applied. It is very different from the technique of dusting sugar flowers, where the paste is dry and the colour does not adhere so readily. When dusting stencil designs, the surface is still wet, thus allowing a larger proportion of colour to be retained. You will find that once the powder colour has been applied to the stencil surface it is very difficult to brush on any additional colour. Try and think ahead and plan the order of colour application, as it is difficult to make good any obvious mistake, and the whole process needs to be done reasonably quickly before the paste dries out. I usually work from a colour drawing as a guide. Always dust on the paler shades first and finish with the darkest areas.

I have mainly used white mexican paste for stencil work, as I find that paler background colours usually give more vibrant contrasts. This does not mean that different base colours cannot be used, however, as darker shades can have striking results. The great

advantage with stencilled decorations is that if you make a mistake whilst colouring up, you only need to replace your plaque or cut-out and do not have to re-cover the whole cake.

It is difficult to avoid some accidental merging of colour. Only by the continuous cleaning or changing of the brush for each colour, and with a little practice, can it be cut down to a minimal amount. However, the occasional wayward overlapping of colours does have its own appeal. In some designs I deliberately accentuate this action by using the same brush and not necessarily cleaning it between shades. This technique creates some unusual tones and seems to enrich the quality of the work overall.

Left: Collect an assortment of cards, pictures, sketches and drawings so that you have a library of ideas and images.

Christmas on the Christmas cake (page 36) to give a three-dimensional effect, and also added some individually piped snowflake lace pieces to balance the overall design.

The use of bas-relief and modelling generates three dimensional life into stencil design. The novelty tomato cake is a good example of this, displaying an occasional modelled pip on top of the flat stencilled ones, and with additional stencil cut-out slices alongside.

A stencil shape is also very flexible. By gently manipulating your design before it dries hard, it will, when applied to the cake and supported while it dries, lift up from the surface of the cake to stunning effect. In the tiered wedding cake (page 74) the flowing shape was created by allowing the stencil to dry in its own way – to move at will. The design is then echoed with the continuing stencil lace pieces. Alternatively, a stencil can be incorporated once it is rigid, having been dried flat or pre-shaped on another surface.

A pre-dried stencil can also be made into an independent three-dimensional piece of work, such as a butterfly (page 49) or a box ornament such as a christening crib for the centrepiece of a cake. (Care must be taken while handling though, as the stencil surface must not be fingered too much – it smudges very easily.) The floating fish (page 38) are a good example of this attractive technique. Finally, the introduction of special decorative techniques such as ragging and sponging adds a new dimension to the cake without distracting from the main stencil feature.

Whatever the technique, presentation is extremely important. You can present your cake as a completely designed work by carrying the style and colour theme through onto the board or board edge – covering it with either matching material or with sugarpaste of an appropriate colour.

COMBINING STENCILLING WITH OTHER SUGARCRAFT TECHNIQUES

A stencil decoration on a cake will capture any observer's attention. The clearly defined shapes and patterns of colour make a very specific statement, and little else in the way of accompaniment is needed. I do use simple painting techniques to enhance the stencil design, as with the fine brush-work on the stencilled flower head on the Mother's Day cake (page 70), adding depth to the arrangement. Another effective but simple addition is pipe-work, such as delicately piped details on figures. I piped a moustache and beard onto the Father

Simple Stencil Plaques and Cut-Outs

A stencilled plaque is probably the best form of introduction to using the stencilling technique. In this chapter I give two examples. The first, a simple celebration cake, has the plaque placed directly onto the iced cake. The second, a novelty tomato cake, shows the plaque being inlaid into the top surface to create a convincing cut tomato face. In each cake the basic method is exactly the same – the difference is merely the way in which both have been incorporated into the overall design.

You can use any stencil in this simple way if you like; rather than cutting out the coloured shape in detail, just trim around the edge to frame it neatly and place directly onto the cake. Extra details can be painted and piped directly onto the image once it has been colour-stencilled, to further enhance the quality of the finished picture.

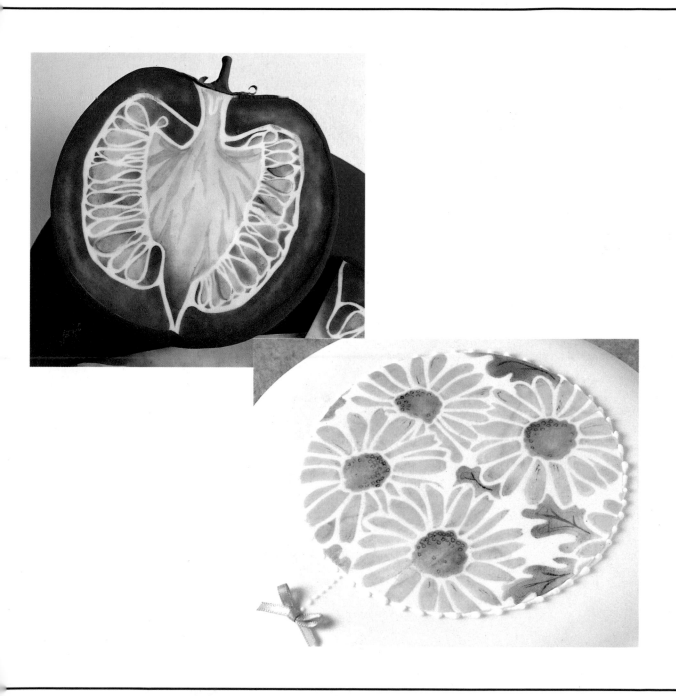

Simple Celebration Cake
for any Occasion

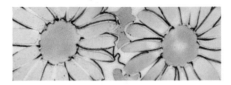

This is the quickest and simplest way of using a stencil, cut into a tile-like flat plaque that can then be placed upon a finished cake. Several small plaques in various colours could even be made up in advance at your convenience and stored until required for an instant but beautiful cake. Making

several of these together is also far more convenient and economical than the occasional one-off.

Simple, effective designs can be easily assembled from greetings cards or magazines. It is worth saving any that inspire you. In this example I chose a daisy pattern for its crisp and fresh qualities.

REQUIREMENTS:

1 round cake, 18 cm (7″)
1 round cakeboard, 23 cm (9″)
450 g (1 lb) marzipan
450 g (1 lb) rolled fondant
    (sugarpaste)
150 g (5 oz) mexican paste
royal icing
dusting colours: yellow, orange
    and green
paste colours: yellow and green
cornflour (cornstarch)
clear alcohol, e.g. vodka
ribbon

DECORATING TIME:
1 day

1 Mix up pale yellow fondant and cover the cakeboard; allow to dry. Cover the cake in marzipan and the same colour fondant and position onto the prepared cakeboard, smoothing out any identations. Make up the acetate stencil in the usual way (see page 9), wash and dry flat. Roll out the mexican paste and prepare the stencil for dusting as described on page 10.

2 Dust the daisy heads in delicate shades of yellow (mix the colour with a little cornflour), slightly edging with a little orange.

3 Dust in the green areas.

4 Remove excess colour with a puffer and then carefully peel off the acetate.

5 Lay a circular card template over your stencil and cut around the edge to make a plaque. Paint details onto the flowers and leaves with a fine brush and a mixture of green paste colour and alcohol. The plaque can be placed immediately onto the cake top or left to dry and secured later (thus allowing it to be removed when the cake is cut, if required).

To complete the cake, pipe a small white snail trail around the edge of the stencil and
base of the cake, using a no. 1 tube. Attach ribbon and bows.

Tomato Cake

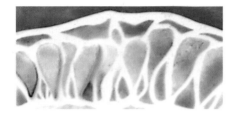

This unusual cake allows the stencilling technique to be used in a quite distinctive manner. It has been incorporated as the entire face of the design; the simple addition of three-dimensional pips and extra slices increases the impact of this effective and light-hearted cake. This cake was designed for a good friend of mine who takes great pride in showing off his large and succulent home-grown tomatoes. I would suggest using a fairly firm cake in order to achieve a neat finish.

REQUIREMENTS:

½ ball-shaped cake, 15 cm (6″)
1 round cakeboard, 25 cm (10″)
350–450 g (¾–1 lb) marzipan
450 g (1 lb) red rolled fondant
   (sugarpaste)
100–150 g (4–5 oz) mexican paste
flower (gum) paste
dusting colours: yellow, green and
   red
paste colours: red and green
cornflour (cornstarch)
clear alcohol, e.g. vodka
green stickyback plastic

DECORATING TIME:
2 days

1 Once the cake has been baked and cooled, slice the top edge off to make the surface level. Trace the basic outline of the tomato stencil pattern onto greaseproof paper; cut out and place onto the flat surface of the cake. Holding firmly with one hand, cut away the excess cake around the pattern. Cover completely with a thin layer of marzipan and allow to dry overnight.

Make up the acetate stencil in the usual way (see page 9), wash and dry flat. Roll out the mexican paste and prepare the stencil for dusting as described on page 10.

Begin dusting in the centre of the tomato stencil with the paler shades, mixing the red powder with cornflour, and work outwards. Now colour the pip areas in a mixture of reds, greens and yellows, blending the colours together a little. Dust the outer edge of the tomato flesh in a deep red and gradually soften the tone as it comes inwards.

2 Remove excess dust colour with a puffer and carefully peel off the stencil from the bottom of the design upwards.

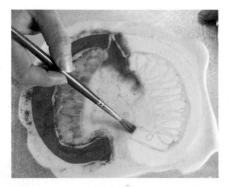

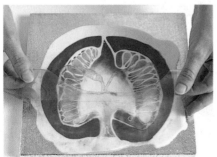

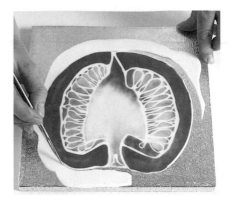

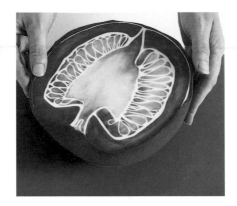

3 Cut around the outer edge of the coloured pattern, leaving a thin margin, and allow to dry on a flat surface. The darker streaks in the centre of the tomato are then painted with a thin brush and a mixture of red paste colour and alcohol.

4 Roll out the red fondant and cover the cake, trimming but leaving a little extra around the flat edge. Smooth off.

5 Place the stencil onto the flat area of the cake, handling as little as possible, and gently ease the fondant over the edge to cover the white margin.

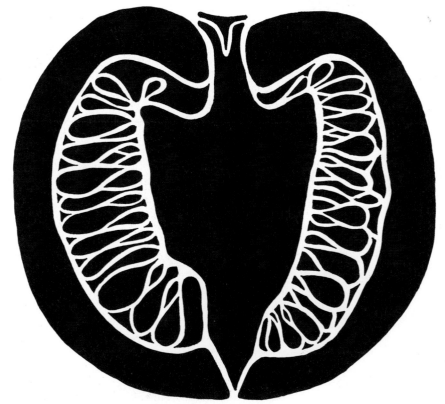

6 To complete the effect, make extra pips using small pieces of painted paste and fix to the surface with egg white or royal icing. This will give a slightly three-dimensional effect. Colour a little flower paste green and make up a calyx to stick onto the tomato. Then, roll out a small stem in green and attach when dry.

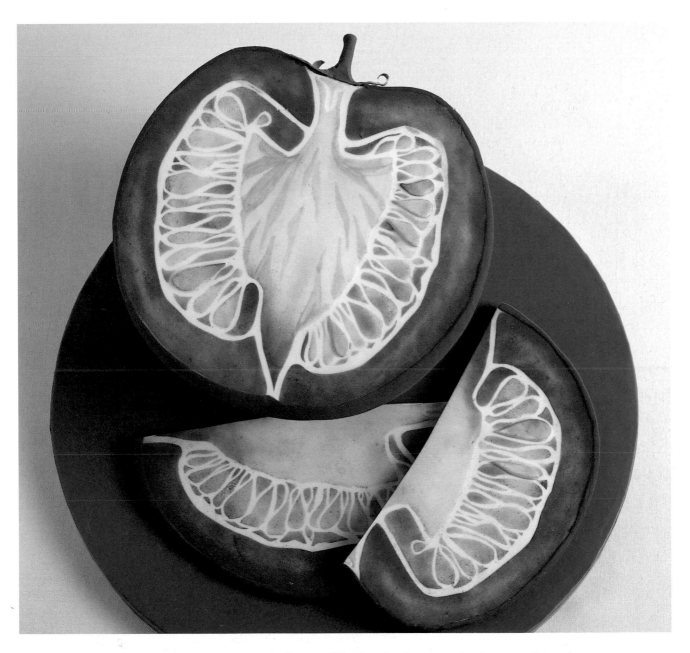

To finish off the cake, repeat the stencilling instructions to make the extra slices of fondant tomato. Place on a thin layer of red fondant, easing over the edges, and cut in half. Cover the cakeboard in green stickyback plastic, place the cake on the board and arrange the slices on the side.

Stencilled Collars

In this chapter I have given two step-by-step examples. The teddy cake shows the more conventional idea of a collar circling the cake in one complete section. The collar on the grape-vine cake, however, has been built up in pieces that overlap each other when they are assembled on the cake. The same amount of care should be taken when handling these pieces as when applying a traditional run-out collar, preferably allowing two to three days' drying time to avoid unnecessary breakages.

Teddy Christening Cake

I have chosen to escape from a typical theme of cribs, bibs and booties and use something a little more informal for this christening cake. The teddies have been designed to hold onto the hoop in different ways, clutching their balloons in an irregular fashion. I have also introduced the technique of ragging, as I feel it complements the design, taking the plainness away from the cake surface without distracting from the main feature. The finely piped balloon strings enrich the overall design.

REQUIREMENTS:

1 round cake, 20 cm (8″)
1 round cakeboard, 28 cm (11″)
675 g (1½ lb) marzipan
675 g (1½ lb) rolled fondant (sugarpaste)
350 g (12 oz) mexican paste
royal icing
dusting colours: lilac, victoria plum, pink and cream
paste colours: claret, brown and black
cornflour (cornstarch)
clear alcohol, e.g. vodka
ribbon

DECORATING TIME:
4 days

1 Cover the cakeboard with fondant and allow to dry overnight. Marzipan and cover the cake with fondant and place on the prepared board, smoothing out any indentations where necessary. Allow plenty of time to dry.

Mix up a very thin consistency of claret paste colour and clear alcohol on a plate. Scrunch up a moistened cloth and dip it into the colour. Before working directly on the cake test out the ragging on a sheet of paper to check the colour consistency. If the effect is too strong, add a little more alcohol.

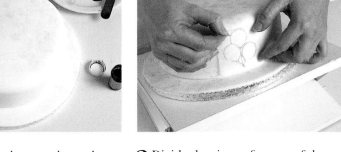

2 Carefully rag the complete cake and board surfaces, varying the density of the colour slightly as you go. This will not take long to dry as the alcohol evaporates quickly.

Next, trace out the name required and transfer onto the cake. Pipe the outline with pale pink icing and a no. 0 tube, allowing it to dry thoroughly before filling in the letterwork with white run-out icing.

3 Divide the circumference of the cake into thirds. Trace the outline of the individual bunches of balloons onto the cake (3 at regular intervals). This is done by scratching with a pin through a traced drawing onto the icing.

4 Pipe over the scratched balloon design outlines in white using a no. 00 tube. Finish them off by attaching a small pink bow onto each bunch of balloons.

Next, pipe a simple scalloped edge round the board in white icing using a no. 0 tube, and secure a piece of pink ribbon around the base of the cake.

5 Make up the acetate stencils in the usual way (see page 9), cutting 2 separate stencils for the collar and the bear with balloons. Wash and dry flat. Roll out the mexican paste and prepare the collar stencil for dusting as described on page 10.

Begin to dust on the colour, starting with the teddies in cream. Dust in the bow ties and the balloons in different shades of pinks and purples toned down with cornflour. Colour the hoop in rich pink. If you intend to do a different colour scheme to the example given here, make sure that you work out which colours go where in advance, as once a mistake is made it is extremely difficult to rectify.

Remove excess dust with a puffer and check that all the areas have been covered before removing the stencil.

Once the acetate has been removed there will no satisfactory way of applying further colour.

6 Remove the acetate and cut around the stencil, slightly bevelling the edge so that it does not appear too heavy. Do not forget to cut out the gaps in between the bears and the hoop as shown in the photograph. Leave to dry for at least 2 or 3 days on a flat porous surface.

7 Repeat the same stencilling process to make the individual teddies for the side of the cake, but rolling the paste out a lot thinner than for the collar. When they have been cut out, apply and secure directly onto the side with royal icing, spacing them equally in between the piped balloons. Bend each piece round to fit the curvature of the cake.

Paint the details (eyes, nose, mouth, etc.) onto all the stencils in brown paste colour mixed with a little alcohol, using a fine paintbrush. Pipe on the balloon strings in black, using a no. 00 tube. Remove the entire collar carefully from the board by sliding off the edge onto the cake and secure with royal icing.

Shades of pink have been used in this cake for a baby girl, although of course the colours can be adapted. I have for example also coloured this stencil design in a rainbow of colours and used it for a birthday cake.

Celebration Cake
for a Private View

This time the collar is made in several segments and then built up and overlapped to very strong effect. The deep burgundy grapes situated beneath the vine leaves continue the colour theme of the leaf tips and lace pieces. When building up a collar, as here, it is important to allow plenty of time for the pieces to dry between stages. Four days decorating time is specified for this project.

REQUIREMENTS:

1 square cake, 20 cm (8″)
1 square cakeboard, 28 cm (11″)
900 g (2 lb) marzipan
900 g (2 lb) ivory rolled fondant
   (sugarpaste)
225–350 g (8–12 oz) mexican paste
royal icing
dusting colours: green, plum and
   white
paste colours: burgundy and
   green
cornflour (cornstarch)
clear alcohol, e.g. vodka
ribbon

DECORATING TIME:
4 days

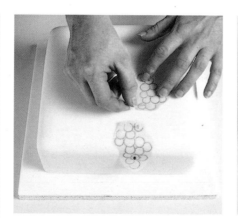

1 Cover the cakeboard with ivory fondant and leave to dry overnight. Marzipan and fondant the cake and place onto the prepared board. Smooth out any indentations.
   Trace the outline of the bunches of grapes onto the cake. This is done by scratching with a pin through a traced drawing onto the icing.

2 Mix up a small amount of burgundy mexican paste. Take a small piece of paste, roll into a ball in the centre of your hand, and flatten one side by pressing gently onto a board. Position it over the scratched design and attach with royal icing or egg white. Continue to build up the bunch of grapes, overlapping in some areas.
   Once the grapes have been completed, if you wish to write anything onto the cake, now is the time to do so.

3 Make up the acetate stencils in the usual way (see page 9), cutting separate stencils. Wash and dry flat. Roll out the mexican paste and prepare the stencils for dusting as described on page 10.

Dust up the 4 corner segments in green mixed with a small amount of cornflour to vary the density of colour. When dusting up the other leaves you can begin to introduce a little plum colour.

4 Remove excess dust with a puffer and carefully peel off the acetate. Cut out each piece as you make it, and repeat this procedure to make 4 of A, 1 of B, 1 of C and 1 of D. Slightly bevel the edges as you cut them so that they do not appear too clumsy – this is done by holding the craft knife at a slight 45° angle. Allow the pieces to dry on a flat porous surface.

5 Attach 2 corner pieces, one on the top right of the cake, the other on the diagonally opposite corner. Secure with a small amount of royal icing. Lay the other 2 segments on the opposite corners, supporting them with sponge until they are dry.

Continue, keeping to a regular pattern.

6 Trace out the lace onto a sheet of paper. Place on a board and cover with clingfilm, wax paper or cellophane and pipe over at least 15 pieces in burgundy royal icing with a no.0 or 00 tube. When they are dry, position and secure onto the cakeboard with a spot of royal icing. Pipe the leaf stems and trail the tendrils haphazardly down the cake.

Finish off by piping a green scalloped line around the board. Brush the grapes with white powder colour and alcohol to make them shine and to create a more three-dimensional effect.

Ribbon Collars

I have provided stencil designs for these two simple and effective collars, as they can be used for many cakes in different ways. As an example I have shown one here being used to conceal the edge of a plaque that is to be inserted into the top of a christening cake. The plaque, once removed after cutting the cake, can be framed in a deep-set frame and kept as a memento of the occasion. I give patterns for both a round and a square design as these are always useful for finishing off a cake.

Stencils Mounted on Curved Surfaces

This is a fairly straightforward and effective use of a stencil that, despite appearances, is quite quick and easy to apply. The length of the stencil is most important as there is a limit to how long a piece of flexible icing one can successfully transfer from the rolling board to the side of the cake. In this chapter I give two examples of its use: the Christmas cake is the simplest, with the stencil secured flat onto the surface. The fish project however pre-forms the stencil shape before it is attached, with rather charming results.

Christmas Cake

This is a rather dazzling Christmas cake that has been designed as an attempt to escape from the traditional snow scene. The bold colours are bright and jolly and fun to use. Inspiration for other images and designs can be drawn from Christmas cards and illustrations: holly and Christmas trees would be ideal subjects to utilize in a stencil. The lace snowflakes have been used to enhance the design, and are piped individually and directly onto the cake at random intervals.

REQUIREMENTS:

1 round deep cake, 20 or 23 cm
   (8 or 9")
1 round cakeboard, 28 cm (11")
450 g (1 lb) marzipan
675 g (1½ lb) red rolled fondant
   (sugarpaste)
225 g (8 oz) mexican paste
royal icing
dusting colours: a wide range
paste colours: black, plus a wide
   range
cornflour (cornstarch)
clear alcohol, e.g. vodka
ribbon

DECORATING TIME:
2 Days

1 Cover the cakeboard in red fondant and leave to dry. (Note: when rolling out dark-coloured fondant icing you must try and avoid using icing sugar as it is difficult to remove the evidence. I wipe a minute amount of white fat on my rolling pin and work surface instead.) Marzipan and fondant the cake and place it centrally onto the prepared cakeboard.
Attach double rows of green ribbon across the cake, and secure on a bow or rosette.

Trace the design onto acetate using a black waterproof pencil or pen. Carefully cut out the stencil, wash and dry flat. Roll out the mexican paste and prepare the stencil for dusting in the usual way (see page 10). Make sure you have a full range of colours ready to use as there is rather a lot of colouring in this particular design.

2 Colouring up should not take more than 5 minutes or the paste will begin to dry. Begin by colouring the paler areas such as the pinks and yellows. Then methodically use each colour across the stencil, cleaning or changing your brush between each shade. Check thoroughly that you have not missed any areas. This can be done by referring to your coloured photograph or diagram.

3 Remove excess dust with a puffer and peel off the stencil. Quickly but carefully cut around the stencil with a craft knife. Cut out white rounds for the bobbles of the hats; these have not been drawn onto the design since they needed to be left white while stencilling.

4 When the pattern has been cut out, place the Christmas cake on a tilt board and carefully transfer the stencil to the side of the cake. Pin up for initial support and secure with royal icing on the reverse side; to avoid smudging try not to move your fingertips across the face of the stencil. Leave to dry.

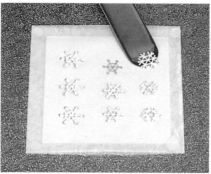

5 Paint on the finer details of Father Christmas and his workers, such as their faces, creases in their clothes, etc. Use a very fine paintbrush and a mixture of co-ordinating paste colours and alcohol. Dust the cheeks of the workers and Father Christmas in pink. Finally, pipe on details such as the hat bobbles, beard and eyebrows, to give a little extra three-dimensional appeal.

6 Trace 10 of each of the snowflake lace pieces onto paper. Place on a board and cover with cellophane, wax paper or clingfilm. Pipe over each piece with white royal icing, using a no. 0 tube. Transfer carefully to the cake with a spatula and secure on with spots of royal icing.

7 Finally, to complete the decoration, pipe snowflakes and spots of snow directly onto the cake using a no. 0 tube. Attach a further piece of ribbon around the edge of the cakeboard.

The finished frieze of Father Christmas and his elves looks deceptively complicated
and intricate; in fact, once the stencil has been cut out, the painting is a painless process
and creates a beautiful effect.

Fish Cake

My aim here is to make the fish appear as though they are swimming around the cake by attaching them to the cake side but leaving a small gap between the cake and the stencil. The simplicity of colouring and paintwork gives style to the cake.

This cake shows a more adventurous way of applying a pre-shaped stencil. A lot of planning is required in order to have three sections of stencil-work overlapping each other, as each section has to be made, shaped and dried separately on the side of the cake. I have incorporated several other techniques to enhance the design, such as the appliqué for the fish fins, the painted details and the subtly piped bubbles of various sizes.

REQUIREMENTS:

1 oval cake, 15 × 23 cm (6 × 9″)
1 oval cakeboard, 23 × 30 cm
    (9 × 12″)
675 g (1½ lb) marzipan
675 g (1½ lb) rolled fondant
    (sugarpaste)
100–175 g (4–6 oz) mexican paste
royal icing
dusting colours: blue, blue-green,
    red and orange
paste colours: blue-green, orange
    and black
cornflour (cornstarch)
clear alcohol, e.g. vodka
ribbon

DECORATING TIME:
at least 4 days

1 Mix up pale aqua-coloured fondant (use a little blue-green colour) and cover the cakeboard. Leave to dry. Cover the cake in marzipan and aqua fondant and transfer onto your prepared cakeboard, smoothing out any indentations. Make up the acetate stencils in the usual way (see page 9), wash and dry flat. Roll out the mexican paste and prepare the stencil for dusting as described on page 10. It is important to roll the mexican paste quite thin, otherwise it may appear too heavy and be difficult to support around the cake.

Colour up the fish as follows: begin with the paler areas of blue, adding cornflour to the colours, and work towards the darker shades. Repeat with red and aqua colours and finally dust the fins with orange.

2 Remove excess dust with a puffer and carefully peel off the acetate. Cut around the fish with a craft knife, allowing a thin margin similar to that of the bridges on the stencil. Take care not to cut too much away as the whole structure will become too delicate to handle. This process needs to be completed reasonably quickly before the paste begins to dry. You will need 3 fish stencils in all, but make and position one at a time.

3 Put the cake on a tilt board and pin a strip of greaseproof paper aound the sides of the cake. Carefully transfer your fish onto the paper, position round and support with pins where necessary. Allow to dry thoroughly, preferably overnight.

Then, mark the position of both ends of the stencilled fish onto the cake and remove from the cake. Turn the cake round to the next starting point, and repeat this process 2 more times with the next 2 fish stencils.

4 When all the pieces are made and dried into their different curves, position them carefully in place on the cake side and attach with small amounts of royal icing piped onto the backs, supporting with pins until dry. Attach the remaining sections, overlapping where necessary. (Make sure you know where each section should go before commencing!) Repeat all these stages for the fish stencil that is to go on top of the cake, but attach when dry as it should lie flat.

6 Cut out and model tiny fins for the larger fish from orange paste, and make a number of tiny eyes, which can be painted with black paste colour. Secure the eyes, and fins at a slight angle, onto the cake with a spot of royal icing.

Pipe irregular-sized bubbles randomly over the surface of the cake and cakeboard using a no. 0 tube. To finish off the decoration, pipe a white snail trail around the base of the cake and attach a complementary-coloured ribbon.

5 Next paint further details onto the fins using a mixture of paste colour and alcohol.

This cake has been decorated in a more feminine way using soft pastel tones. If it is to be for a man, however, a bolder approach to colouring would be more appropriate.

Introducing Painting Textures

Nothing can be simpler than ragging or sponging colour onto a cake: depending on the type of materials and the way they are used, an almost endless variety of decorative effects can be achieved. It is best to experiment to begin with. When you have found a pattern or combination that you like, you can apply it to your cake surface. I use these techniques to decorate several cakes in this book, not necessarily keeping to one shade.

A sponged or ragged surface is effective as a background to a stencil design, providing overall even colouring and taking the plainness away without distracting the eye from a central feature, for instance a spray of flowers. Experiment with materials to add depth to your work: a piece of cotton, for example, would produce a slightly different effect to that of muslin.

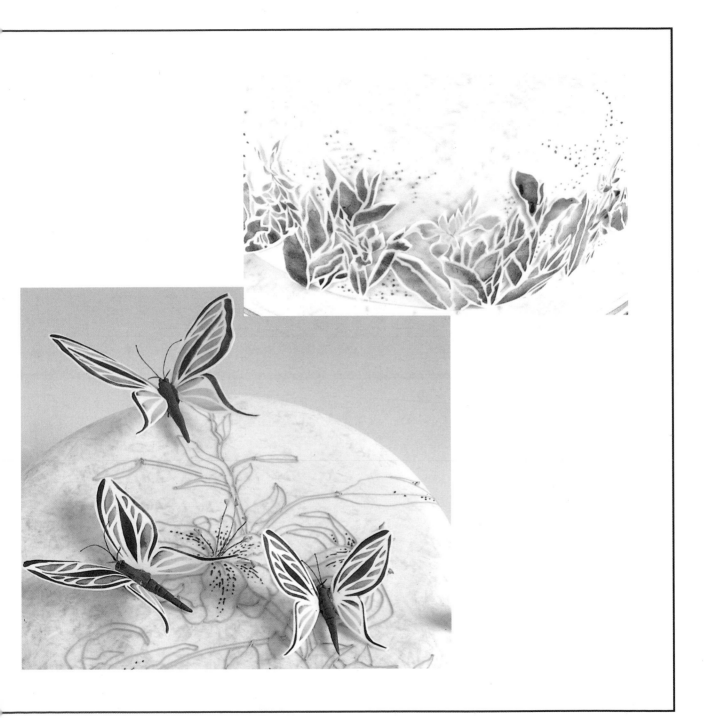

21st Birthday Cake

This is a rather intricately cut stencil but it is used in a very simple fashion. It has a multitude of colours blended together in quite an accidental way. This is a good example of how colours can be merged together simply by dragging residue dust across the stencil surface. The variegated sponged background in pale grape violet shades is complementary and subtle enough to soften the rather hard edge of the stencil design. It may be helpful to practice the sponging technique on a sheet of paper.

REQUIREMENTS:

1 round cake, 20 cm (8")
1 round cakeboard, 25 cm (10")
675 g (1½ lb) marzipan
675 g (1½ lb) rolled fondant
    (sugarpaste)
175 g (6 oz) mexican paste
royal icing
paste colours: violet, green and
    orange
dusting colours: greens, blues,
    red, orange, yellow, violet and
    damson
natural marine sponge
clear alcohol, e.g. vodka

**DECORATING TIME:
2–3 days**

1 Cover the cakeboard in white fondant and leave to dry. Marzipan and fondant the cake and place onto the prepared cakeboard. Smooth out any indentations.

Mix together a thin consistency of alcohol and violet paste colour. Evenly sponge the cake surface and board. Take care when sponging at the base of the cake as this area does not want to become too dark.

2 Make up the acetate stencils in the usual way (see page 9), wash and dry flat. Roll out the mexican paste and prepare the main border stencil for dusting as described on page 10.

Dust in the usual manner, commencing with the paler shades. Certain areas such as the reds, oranges and yellows need to be dusted with a clean brush every time. The shades can be merged a little into each other.

3 When all the colouring has been completed, remove the excess dust with a puffer and carefully peel off the acetate. Cut out the stencil pattern all the way round with a craft knife, including in between some of the stem area. Do not cut away too much as it may then be too delicate to transfer onto the cake.

4 Place the cake on a tilt board and carefully position the stencil onto the side. This is quite an awkward procedure. It must be done as soon as the stencil has been completely cut out. Once it has been transferred, support immediately with pins and secure with royal icing on the reverse.

Make another 2 of these sections and secure in the same way, overlapping each section a little.

TEXTURED PAINTING

REQUIREMENTS:

clear alcohol, e.g. gin or vodka

range of edible paste colours

materials for pouncing – natural marine sponge, muslin, paper, polythene or plastic bag

It is not essential to leave your sugarpaste covering to harden before beginning textured painting.

You only need to use a gentle touch to imprint the design of the cloth onto your cake. If you find you are creating indentations on the cake surface simply lighten the pressure.

Whatever texture of material you use, the technique is exactly the same. Simply mix up a thin consistency of clear alcohol and paste colour on a plate. Dampen your sponge or thin cotton cloth with water and wring out thoroughly. Scrunch up the material, arranging the padding surface. You will find that a tighter pad will make a more definite line, whereas a loosely scrunched cloth will make more solid areas of colour. Test on a piece of paper first. Dab the material into the colour mixture, working it evenly into the pad, and then proceed to 'pounce' it onto the prepared surface. Be careful not to get carried away as only a light touch of colour is needed to create a subtle effect.

A combination of colours can be merged together to create unusual shades, as displayed in the tiger lily and butterfly cake. Plan your colours carefully to co-ordinate with the rest of the design.

5 Colour up the ribbon stencil for the top of the cake; once the pattern has been cut out, leave to dry, lifting and supporting parts of the ribbon with sponge pieces.

6 Pipe the outline of 21 onto the top of the cake in green with a no. 0 tube, and then pipe the remaining embroidery detail onto the rest of the cake.

To finish off, fill in the 21 with purple run-out royal icing and attach the ribbon stencil carefully with a spot of royal icing. Tie a complementary ribbon around the cakeboard to complete the effect.

Tiger Lily and Butterfly Cake

Butterflies are a lovely subject to work with, and can be incorporated in many ways. They are sometimes featured on wedding cakes amongst a spray of flowers or as a lace addition to balance a particular design. The intricate network of colours and designs are simplified with the use of a stencil. I have not attempted to make them look life-like; I am simply interpreting them in stencil form. The tiger-lilies have been piped directly on the cake surface in a simple outline. A partially three-dimensional approach has been introduced by using cotton stamens to tie together the outlined imagery.

I have tried to develop this theme with a masculine feel to it, as I find it very difficult to avoid decorating a cake that includes flowers and butterflies without making it too pretty. I have blended shades of deep green and black with touches of yellow and orange to accomplish this effect.

REQUIREMENTS:

1 round cake, 23 cm (9″)
1 round cakeboard, 30 cm (12″)
675–900 g (1½–2 lb) marzipan
900 g (2 lb) ivory rolled fondant
    (sugarpaste)
flower (gum) paste
royal icing
paste colours: yellow, green, black
    and orange
dusting colours: orange, yellow,
    green and black
clear alcohol, e.g. vodka
egg white
green and black stamens
28-gauge wire
ribbon

DECORATING TIME:
2–3 days

1 Cover the cakeboard in ivory fondant and leave to dry. Cover the cake with marzipan and the remaining icing and place onto the prepared cakeboard, smoothing out any indentations. Allow to dry. Mix up a thin consistency of alcohol and yellow paste colour and rag approximately a third of the cake surface, leaving the rest ivory.

2 Mix a small amount of green paste into the present yellow mixture, add a little more alcohol and continue to rag a little further over the cake surface, overlapping into the yellow areas. Finally, rag the remaining area in a darker green, again overlapping colours slightly. Allow to dry.

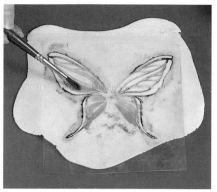

3 Trace the lily pattern and transfer onto the cake surface by scratching through the surface of the paper with a pin. Pipe over the entire scratched drawing in royal icing, using shades of orange and green (include a green snail trail around the base of the cake at this stage).

Pipe black specks onto the flower centres. Paint a little black paste colour onto green stamen cotton stems and insert into the centre of the flowers, securing them with a small amount of egg white.

4 Make up the 4 individual acetate butterfly stencils in the usual way (see page 9), wash and dry flat. Instead of using mexican paste I have used flower paste as it can be rolled out much thinner and dries a lot quicker, which is essential when assembling butterflies (making them too thick would result in difficulty in supporting the wings when attaching to the main body). Roll out your flower paste and prepare the stencils for dusting as described for mexican paste on page 10.

Colour up the stencils using a small soft brush. Begin by dusting the paler areas, i.e. yellow and orange, then clean or change your brush and continue dusting in the green and black areas.

5 When everything has been coloured remove the excess dust with a puffer and carefully peel off the acetate. Cut out each wing with a sharp craft knife and dry on a flat porous surface.

little. Cut it so that it is smaller than the width of the main body and secure to the underside of the body with a mixture of egg white and flower paste. At the same time insert 2 pairs of legs made with 28-gauge wire, one pair slightly longer than the other. Position and secure with egg white and flower paste onto the under-body, with the longer pair positioned at the front.

When the wings are competely dry attach them onto the little shelf edge with egg white/flower paste mixture, and support at once with foam squares. When dry, paint the body to accentuate the ridge marks on the body, using black food colour diluted with some clear alcohol.

6 Now assemble the butterflies. Mix up a small amount of dark grey flower paste. For each butterfly, take a pea-sized piece to make the body section. Roll into a ball, place into the palm of your hand and roll one end to form a long pointed sausage shape. Ridge the body with the back edge of a knife. On each side of the body near the head press a knife side against the body to create a little shelf.

7 Next, make a pin-hole in the centre of the head to position the antennae (fine black cotton stamens). Roll another tiny piece of paste into the palm of your hand and flatten it a

8 Make all 4 butterflies in exactly the same way, taking time and great care. Here I show some other butterfly shapes and colours to demonstrate the versatility of colour and design. If making larger wings, increase the body size to correspond.

On the completed cake, the butterflies have been positioned onto the cake top and secured with egg white and flower paste mixture. The base of the cake and the cakeboard have been decorated with ribbon.

Inlaid Stencils

Unfortunately stencils cannot be used directly as a form of cake covering. If the decoration were done on sugarpaste and then wrapped over the surface of the cake, stretching would distort the image and the loose colours would make it impossible to smooth the icing. Inlaid stencils are the nearest alternative way in which stencils can become part of the surface decoration. (They can also be laid directly on top of the cake if you are short of time.) My inspiration has been drawn from the wide range of tiles that I have designed and decorated in the past.

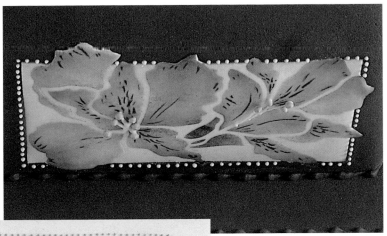

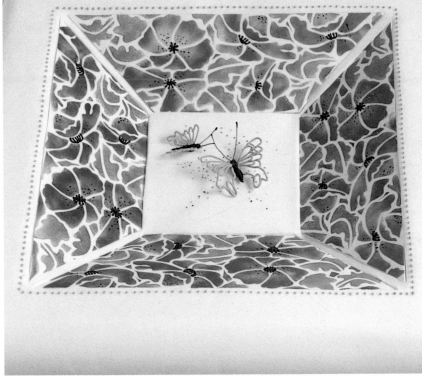

Poppy Cake

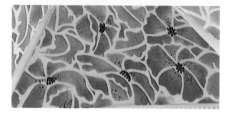

The design of this cake is rather unusual, with a combination of angles and shapes that give a bold but charming effect. Providing the initial shape is cut well, the mounting of the panels will be fairly straightforward. The central panels have been shaped by bevelling the top surface of the cake before covering, to create a picture frame effect. Cut-out corner features enhance the design by breaking up the continuous line. Soft piping is then used to tone down the bright poppy pattern.

REQUIREMENTS:

1 square cake, 23 cm (9″)
1 square cakeboard, 30 cm (12″)
900 g (2 lb) marzipan
900 g (2 lb) rolled fondant
    (sugarpaste)
350–450 g (¾–1 lb) mexican paste
royal icing
paste colours: green and black
dusting colours: blue, green and
    red
jam
clear alcohol, e.g. vodka
black flower stamens

DECORATING TIME:
3–4 days

1 Once the cake has been cooked, allow to cool completely before cutting. Cut a strip of card 2.5 × 23 cm (1 × 9″), hold this template up against the base of the cake and score a line across the top from edge to edge with a sharp knife.
Repeat this process on all 4 sides, making a very definite mark. Turn the cake on its side and cut this section off, following the guidelines that have been marked.

2 Cut diagonally across all 4 corners of the thin wedge you have just made to make 4 triangles.

3 Cut a 6.5 cm (2½") square out of the centre. Make a card template 23 × 5 cm (9 × 2") and score a 23 cm (9") line down the centre. Carefully bend it into a 90° angle. Lay this over the outside edge of each triangle, and holding firmly in place, cut away at an angle to create a bevelled slope. This is done by placing your knife against the card edge and tapering the cut towards the centre. Before you reassemble, fill any holes on the bevelled edges with marzipan, and make sure that the top cake ledges are level.

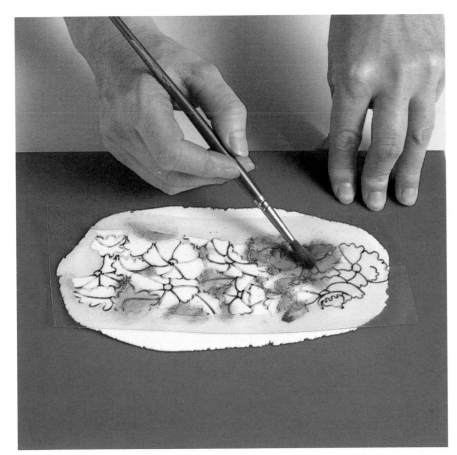

4 Reassemble the 4 pieces back onto the base of the cake, securing with a little jam. Marzipan the centre and the 4 bevelled panels in individual pieces and the remaining sides with another 4 pieces. The cake must be marzipanned in individual sections in order to keep the shape sharply defined. Unlike other cakes, it should not be covered in fondant until the stencilled panels have been made and dried.

Trace the stencil patterns onto individual sheets of acetate, tracing pattern B twice but turning it over for a reverse tracing before cutting again. Wash and dry flat. Roll out a piece of mexican paste and prepare the stencils for dusting in the usual way (see page 10). The paste does not have to be rolled out too thinly; ideally it needs to be a similar thickness to that of the fondant which will cover the cake.

Begin by colouring the blue fill-in areas, shading evenly. Dust in the small amounts of green for the leaves, and finally shade the poppies, varying the density of colour on their petals to give them more depth.

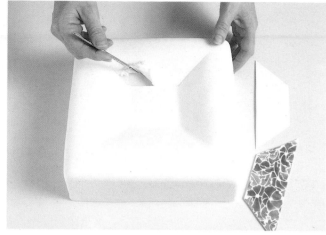

5 When all the areas have been coloured, remove the excess dust with a puffer and carefully peel off the acetate. Trace and cut out a trapezium-shaped card template, lay it over the coloured stencil and, holding firmly but being careful not to smudge, cut round with a craft knife. Make 4 of these panels altogether. Once all the panels have been made, leave them to dry thoroughly. This may take a little longer than usual.

6 Once the panels are dry, the cake can be covered with white fondant icing. Use the same trapezium card template, i.e. the shape of the panel, and lay it on one bevelled surface of the cake. Holding firmly in place, cut out this area with a small craft knife. When you have cut all the way round, lift a corner of the icing with your knife point and gradually peel off this section.

7 Pipe around the inside edge of the space and across the centre with a little royal icing, and carefully position and secure a stencilled panel in place. Do not press so hard that the panel is at a lower level than the fondant icing. If there are any spaces between the panel and the fondant covering, gently ease the fondant icing with a smoothing tool into place to achieve a nice snug fit.

Repeat this process with the remaining 3 panel sections, cutting each area out one by one. (If you are short of time these panels could simply be placed on top of the rolled fondant (sugarpaste) and piped around the edges to neaten.)

8 Make up the 4 corner panels using exactly the same stencilling process. (These can be rolled out a lot thinner.) Make 8 pieces in all, not forgetting that they have to fit opposite corners so you will need to reverse the pattern for half of them. After making each piece, meticulously cut out, and leave to dry on a flat porous surface.

Put the cake on a tilt board and assemble the corner sections, attaching with royal icing. Each piece should interlock with its partner at the corners. Pin where necessary to support the pieces until they are dry. Then, paint on the flower head details and pipe on the poppy seed boxes in black using a no. 00 tube.

9 Trace the pattern of each butterfly onto a sheet of paper, place on a board and cover with a sheet of wax paper or cellophane. Pipe the wings in green royal icing using a no. 0 tube and leave to dry.

To assemble the butterflies, pipe the body in black royal icing using a no. 2 tube. Position each wing onto the body and support at once with foam until dry. Insert 2 fine stamens as antennae and leave to dry.

To complete the cake, pipe the remaining detail onto the cake with a border around the panels and the edge of the cakeboard. Position and secure the butterflies onto the cake with royal icing. Attach a bow.

Alstroemeria Birthday Cake

This cake has a dramatic and contrasting combination of colours, which draws attention to the simple but effective stencilled panels. The design of the inlaid panels is echoed by the single flower placed on top of the cake, which introduces a three-dimensional aspect to the overall design.

REQUIREMENTS:

1 hexagonal cake, 20 cm (8″)
1 hexagonal cakeboard, 25 cm (10″)
675 g (1½ lb) marzipan
675 g (1½ lb) rolled fondant (sugarpaste)
225–300 g (8–10 oz) mexican paste
flower (gum) paste
royal icing
dusting colours: green, red and burgundy
paste colours: burgundy and green
cornflour (cornstarch)
semolina
green cotton stamens
pink stamen cotton
30-gauge wire
white tape

DECORATING TIME:
2–3 days

1 Colour the fondant a burgundy shade. Avoid using any icing sugar, as this will dry out the icing and make it crack. Use a little white fat on your hands if necessary to stop it from sticking. Use a little rolled fondant (sugarpaste) to cover the cakeboard and leave to dry.

Make up the acetate stencil in the usual way (see page 9), wash and dry flat. Roll out the mexican paste and prepare the stencil for dusting as described on page 10. Delicately colour the alstroemeria panel in shades of pink and green, mixing with a little cornflour.

59

2 Remove excess dust with a puffer and carefully peel off the acetate. Lay a rectangular card template over the stencil, hold down firmly so that it doesn't move and cut along the edge, missing the overhanging petal.

Remove the card and cut around the protruding areas of petal, not allowing any margin. Carefully press each petal onto the board surface slightly, so that they do not rise up when they are on the cake. Make 6 of these panels altogether and allow to dry thoroughly.

3 Cover the cake with the remaining burgundy fondant and place onto the prepared cakeboard. Position the rectangular card template on the side of the cake and carefully cut all the way round with a craft knife. (Note that the cake must not be covered until the panels have been made and dried, as it is important to ease the icing against the panel to give a snug fit.)

4 Remove the piece of burgundy icing carefully.

5 Pipe a line of royal icing inside the cut area and secure a stencilled panel in place. Press the protruding petals gently into the soft fondant so that they appear to be inlaid as well.

Ease the burgundy fondant up against the edge of the panel so that there is no gap. Repeat this process for all 6 panels.

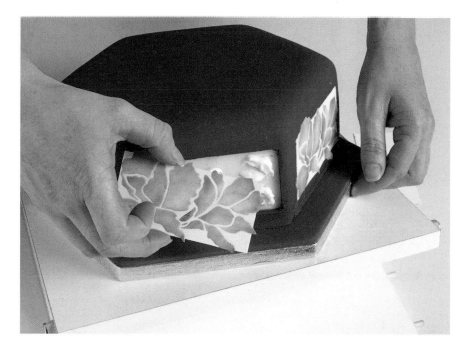

6 Complete the panels by painting details onto the flower heads. Pipe on pink stamens, then decorative dots around the panels, using a no. 0 tube. Use a no. 1 tube to pipe a burgundy snail trail around the base of the cake and edge of the cakeboard.

7 Cut 3 card petal templates. Roll out a piece of pale pink-coloured flower paste using a paint brush, keeping a thicker area towards the centre at one end. Place the petal template over the paste and cut around. Repeat to make 3 large petals in the pink paste, then use off-white and green-coloured paste to make 3 smaller petals and 3 large leaves respectively.

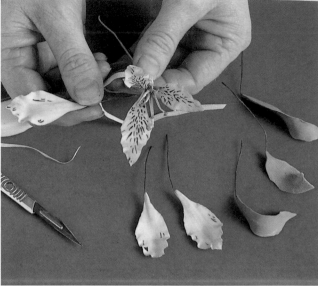

8 Vein the petals, using the back of a real petal or a veining tool, and then place a piece of hooked 30-gauge wire (just dipped in egg white) into the thicker part of each. Dust and paint the flower petals, taking colours and detail from the stencilled panels.

9 To assemble the flower, place the 3 smaller petals around the outside of 6 stamens. Arrange the 3 outer petals in the alternate gaps, tuck the leaves in underneath and tape tightly with white tape to secure everything in position. Dust the stems with green dust to finish.

The completed cake has a special message or greeting piped on in pink royal icing. The alstroemeria is simply placed on top.

Piercing and Cut-Out Work

This aspect of my work gives the greatest scope of all. It is the beginning of the process of making a stencil a three-dimensional feature. Basically, it means that once a stencil has been coloured and the acetate removed, it is then completely cut out. It can then be either immediately attached to the cake surface or left to dry and secured on afterwards. Obviously the more paste that is cut away from the design, the weaker the structure will be. So begin with something simple in order to become familiar with the technique and establish its limits. A collar is probably one of its most common uses. It is best to experiment to begin with. When you have found a pattern or combination that you like and can manage, you can then apply it to your cake surface.

In this chapter I have designed 3 cakes: a clown cake that is basically a simple cut-out with a cleverly tilted head, a Mother's Day cake combined with flower modelling, and a very unusual three-tiered wedding cake which has cut-outs that stand out attached to the edge.

Clown Cake

This is one of my favourite cakes, simple in design and colour, full of fun and fairly quick and easy to make. The use of strong primary colours naturally lends it to a child's birthday cake. The clown's attire is echoed on the background cake with simple piped star shapes outlined in a variety of co-ordinating colours. His carefully lifted head is an additional three-dimensional feature that, together with the ruffled collar and piped details, creates excellent depth and character.

REQUIREMENTS:

1 oval cake, 20 × 25 cm (8 × 10″)
1 oval cakeboard, 25 × 30 cm
    (10 × 12″)
675 g (1½ lb) marzipan
675 g (1½ lb) rolled fondant
    (sugarpaste)
175–225 g (6–8 oz) mexican paste
flower (gum) paste
royal icing
paste colours: black, green, red
    and orange
dusting colours: a wide range
cornflour (cornstarch)
green stickyback plastic, sticky
    shapes

DECORATING TIME:
3 days

1 To begin with I thought it would be fun to co-ordinate the colours by covering the cakeboard in green paper and decorating it with sticky shapes. Then, coat the cake in marzipan and white fondant and leave to dry overnight.

Make up the acetate stencil in the usual way, cutting 2 separate stencils for the clown and the balloon. Do not make the mistake of cutting out the face as this is to remain white. Wash and dry flat. Roll out the mexican paste and prepare the stencil for dusting as described on page 10.

Colour up as shown in the illustration over. Begin with the paler colours such as the pink on the ears (use cornflour with red) and the yellow on the tummy. Clean your brush between each colour in order to achieve crisp, clear shades.

3 Paint the eyes, eyebrows and mouth onto the face with black colour and place onto a piece of wax paper or clingfilm (saran wrap). Pipe on the hair, using a no. 0 tube and orange icing, and his nose in red and leave to dry overnight.

Pipe the name of the child onto the cake in green using a no. 1 tube. Leave until completely dry and later fill in the letters with red run-out icing. Pipe on decorative stars, a message on the balloon as desired, and pipe a decorative white snail trail around the base of the cake.

2 When colouring has been completed, remove excess dust with a puffer and carefully peel off the stencil. Cut around the edge of the clown with a craft knife, allowing a small margin of white similar to that of the bridges in the stencil. Neatly cut off the open hand, head and feet and dry on a flat porous surface.

Repeat this complete process to make the balloon, taking particular care when colouring up to leave it slightly paler towards the centre, so that it appears to shine.

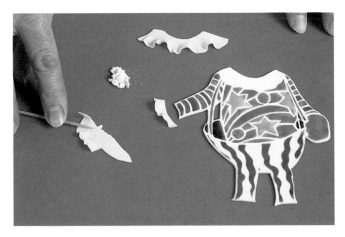

4 Roll out a thin strip of flower paste on a non-stick surface and frill along one edge with a cocktail stick, as you would frill a carnation. Cut 2 lengths for the neck ruffle, and 2 for the sleeves.

5 Place the clown's body onto the cake and secure with royal icing. Position on the ruffles and secure with royal icing. Situate and secure the feet, head, hand and balloon and support immediately with pieces of sponge, tilting each part upwards.

If the idea of separating out the various parts of the clown's body and propping them at an angle seems too complicated, the clown stencil can simply be used to make a decorative plaque for mounting onto a cake.

The finished cake has remaining details piped on in appropriate colours: shoe laces, balloon string, etc.

Mother's Day Cake

This cake combines several techniques. Specific areas are three-dimensional; individual petals have been modelled in flower paste and secured directly onto the stencil surface, and fine cotton stamens have been placed and carefully painted as an additional effect. A hollow underneath the collar emphasizes the remarkably delicate work, and the side panel sections continue the colour theme but have been simplified into a cut-out frieze effect, incorporating an unusual overlap at the front.

REQUIREMENTS:

1 round cake, 20 cm (8″)
1 round cakeboard, 25 cm (10″)
675 g (1½ lb) marzipan
675 g (1½ lb) rolled fondant (sugarpaste)
225–350 g (8–12 oz) mexican paste
flower (gum) paste
royal icing
dusting colours: holly green, red and burgundy
paste colours: burgundy and holly green
jam
egg white
cornflour (cornstarch)
white cotton stamens
ribbon

DECORATING TIME:
4 days

1 Place the cake the right way up and mark a 2 cm (¾″) line all the way round from the bottom of the cake, using a card template. Turn the cake onto its side and cut off this section following the marked guidelines (an electric knife is ideal). Remove the slice and cut a further circle out of its centre, approx. 13 cm (5″) in diameter. Remove the centre piece and replace the rim on the base of the cake, securing with jam.

Cover the cake with one sheet of marzipan, easing it carefully into the hole in the centre, and leave to dry. Cover the cakeboard in fondant and dry overnight. With the remaining fondant cover the cake and place onto the prepared board, smoothing out any indentations.

2 Make up the acetate stencils in the usual way (see page 9), wash and dry flat. (Note that some of the petals of the flower design have been blocked out. This indicates that they should not be cut out, as they will be made individually in flower paste.)

Roll out the mexican paste and prepare the stencil for dusting as described on page 10. Colour up, starting with the green areas first. Take particular care when dusting the flowers as the shading is an important feature of this particular design. Mix in a little cornflour for the paler shades on the petals.

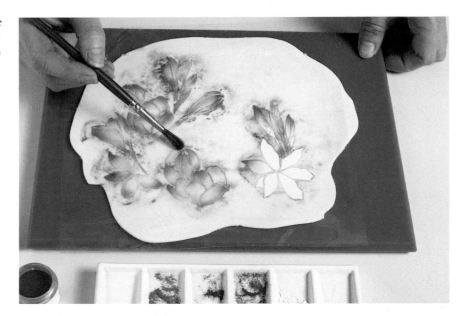

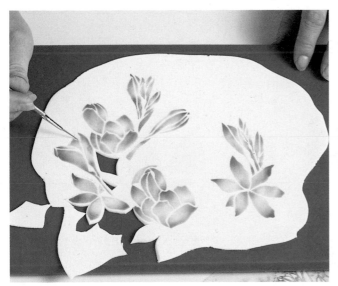

3 When all the colouring has been completed, remove the acetate carefully and cut out the stencil with a craft knife. Paint on extra details using a fine brush.

Insert small white cotton stamens into the appropriate areas, securing them with a little egg white. Leave to dry for at least 2 days on a porous surface.

4 Trace individual petals onto tracing paper and cut out. Make up one petal at a time.

Roll out a very thin piece of flower paste on a non-stick surface, place the petal template over and cut around. Thin out the edge with a cocktail stick and allow to dry.

5 Dust the petals in the same pinks used for the stencil and paint finer details onto each petal. Attach to the ready-made stencil so that they stick up at an angle, securing with royal icing.

6 Make the stencil for the side of the cake in exactly the same way. Once each piece has been made and cut, attach immediately, overlapping at the front and back of the cake (support while drying with foam).

Pipe on the required lettering and around the edge of the board. Secure on the bows.

When the collar is completely dry fix it onto the cake, positioning centrally over the hollow and securing with royal icing.

Three-Tier Wedding Cake

This stunning white wedding cake really makes use of the three-dimensional possibilities of this stencilling technique. The vivid colours of the freesias are echoed in a casually placed bow on the top of the cake, which gives added conviction to a most unusual design. The pierced stencilled sections have been precisely placed, interlocking with each other to create space between each.

This is a reasonably quick cake to decorate. The time-consuming task is cutting out the stencil patterns. Take great care when doing this to avoid unsightly repairs if possible.

REQUIREMENTS:

3 hexagonal cakes, 13 cm (5″),
    18 cm (7″) and 23 cm (9″)
2 hexagonal cakeboards, 13 cm
    (5″) and 18 cm (7″)
1 hexagonal cake drum,
    30 cm (12″)
1.8 kg (4 lb) marzipan
1.8 kg (4 lb) rolled fondant
    (sugarpaste)
6 plastic supports
225–350 g (8–12 oz) mexican paste
dusting colours: red, pinks,
    yellow, purple/plums and green
royal icing
1 metre of each shade of 3 mm
    (⅛″) double-sided satin ribbon

DECORATING TIME:
2–3 days or less

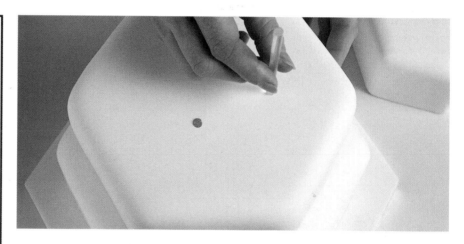

1 Cover the cake drum with white fondant and leave to dry. Place the 2 smaller cakes on their corresponding cakeboards, and the bottom largest cake on the cake drum. Marzipan and fondant the 2 top tiers so that the boards are completely hidden. Marzipan and fondant the bottom tier and place onto the prepared cake drum. Leave to dry.

Cut 3 equal plastic supports for the bottom and middle tiers and insert into each cake. These are used to ensure that the cakes do not sink into each other once tiered. Once this has been done the cakes can be placed on top of each other. Attach a double band of antique white ribbon around the base of each cake with royal icing. Pipe a fine snail trail around the base of each cake.

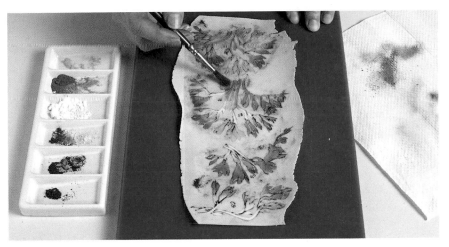

2 Make up the acetate stencil in the usual way (see page 9), wash and dry flat. The sizes of the freesia patterns vary – the larger ones are used at the bottom of the cake and the smaller at the top.

Roll out the mexican paste and prepare the stencil for dusting as described on page 10. Begin with the lighter shades such as the yellow, follow on with the pinks and reds, etc., and finish off with the greens. Your brush does not need to be cleaned thoroughly between each colour but simply brushed on a piece of kitchen towel.

3 Once all the areas have been covered, remove the excess dust with a puffer and carefully peel off the acetate. Cut carefully around the spray of flowers and in between the stems and flower heads. Take care not to cut too much away as the structure will become too delicate to handle. Make 5 of A, 5 of B, 4 of C and 2 of D.

4 Keeping one complete piece each of A, B and C to one side, cut the rest up as each are made into individual 'florets' or pieces. Allow to dry flat overnight on a porous surface. Each spray pattern can be shaded differently so that there is overall variation in the design.

5 Repeat the stencilling process for the small posy (E), varying the colours, but as each one is made place it directly onto the cake on alternate corners, securing with a spot of royal icing. Make 5 in total for the back of the cake. Place a bow on each posy, attaching with royal icing. Paint on accentuating petal lines in matching paste colours and alcohol.

6 Now mount the stencilled panels. Begin at the bottom on a point of the hexagon. Place on the main 2 sprays, slightly overlapping each other, and attach further sprigs so that they interlock with one another. Secure with royal icing.

7 Continue the process on each tier. The pieces may need supporting with pins and foam wedges until they are dry.

To complete the cake, make a casual bow with ribbons of similar colours to those of the
freesias. Curl the long ribbon ends over the back of a knife and secure on with royal
icing; position them slightly off-centre and towards the back of the cake, trailing the
ends down the sides.

Incorporating Cavity Features

Cutting out part of the surface of a cake introduces many exciting possibilities for designing something new. Creating a cavity throws into relief a stencil laid on top and adds to the three-dimensional effect. In this chapter I give two examples that emphasize this feature, although it is used elsewhere in the book in various ways.

When designing a cake that features an unusual cavity area or facet, it is important to have a good basic shape to work from. A firm cake is necessary for carving as anything else may crumble. A clean cut is particularly important if angles are to be incorporated. A very sharp carving knife or an electric knife will give the best results. Also, make sure that your cakes are deep enough where necessary to take some of the more unusual side decorations.

Marzipan-covering your carved cakes is relatively easy to do but requires a little thought before beginning. Decide where the sharp edges and corners are to be kept and where the outside edges have to be covered in a continuous piece in order to give a chamfered finish.

After marzipan, fondant icing has been used to cover each cake in the normal fashion. Simply roll out the required amount on the work surface, lift and lay over the cake surface, easing into the crevices with your fingertips. Smooth off with the use of a plastic smoothing tool.

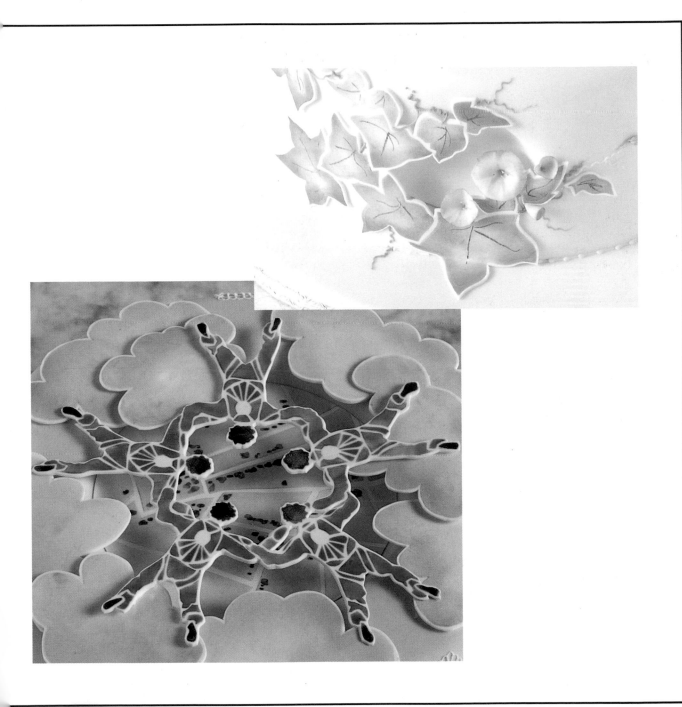

Creeping Ivy and Lace Wedding Cake

This single-tiered wedding cake is a very delicate example of combining stencil patterns with lace work. I have tried to keep the theme as simple as possible, and allowed the ivy to take its own course and impart a feeling of unrestricted growth. The gradual introduction of pink tones in the lace pieces echoes the morning glory, which has been combined with the stencil pattern in a three-dimensional way. The cavities recur around the cake and provide a starting point for the stencils. The fine pipe work is an additional feature that draws the whole design elegantly together.

REQUIREMENTS:

1 deep round cake, 20 cm (8″)
1 round cakeboard, 28 cm (11″)
675 g (1½ lb) marzipan
675 g (1½ lb) ivory rolled fondant
   (sugarpaste)
225–350 g (8–12 oz) mexican paste
flower (gum) paste
royal icing
dusting colours: red and green
paste colours: red and green
cornflour (cornstarch)
clear alcohol, e.g. vodka
egg white
pink flower stamens

DECORATING TIME:
2 days

1 Divide the circumference of the cake into thirds. Cut a circular card template, approx. 6.5 cm (2½″) in diameter, place over the centre of each marked point and score gently with a knife around the card. Do not cut too deeply. Carefully carve out a curved indentation, almost a hemisphere, using a small knife. I have used a grapefruit knife that has a slight bend in the end.

Press a ball shape into the cavity and twist to neaten the cut. Repeat this process two more times around the cake.

2 Marzipan the cake in the usual fashion using one complete piece. Again, press firmly into the cavity areas with a ball, to tidy. Trim the edges at the board.

Cover the cakeboard in ivory fondant and leave to dry. Fondant the cake and place onto the prepared board, smoothing out any indentations.

3 Trace out the lace pieces onto a sheet of paper, place on a board and cover with clingfilm or wax paper. Pipe with a no. 0 or 00 tube and make 5 small, 25 medium and 5 large lace pieces. This should allow enough for any breakages. When piping the medium-sized pieces, begin by using green royal icing, then gradually introduce pink into each piece of lace until eventually the whole section is pink. Allow to dry.

With the remaining pink royal icing, pipe a small snail trail around the base of the cake. Faintly mark a circle 10 cm (4″) in diameter with a pin on the top of the cake.

5 Remove excess dust with a puffer and carefully peel off the acetate. In this particular stencil design, I have divided the pattern into sections. Cut out around the outside of the design and then individually cut out some of the ivy leaves that trail. Try and cut away as much as possible without weakening the structure.

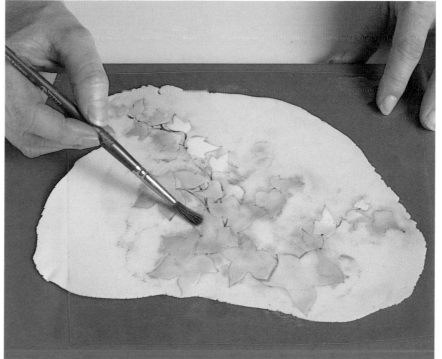

4 Make up the acetate stencil in the usual way (see page 9), wash and dry flat. Roll out the ivory-coloured mexican paste and prepare the stencil for dusting as described on page 10. Use a mixture of green shades and cornflour to dust up the ivy, and create a variegated effect.

6 As soon as the ivy has been cut out, transfer it to the cake which has been placed ready on a tilt board. Lay the ivy directly over the hollow. Pin and attach the stencil in several places with royal icing.

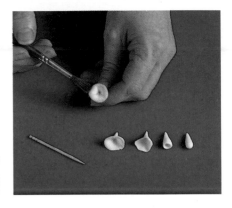

7 Repeat this process with the single leaves, securing with royal icing. Some of the leaves have been supported whilst drying to make them bend and so stand off the cake at a slight angle. Repeat to decorate the remaining cavity areas.

8 Pipe on the ivy stems and tendrils with the remaining green royal icing, using a no.0 or 00 tube, and paint the detail of the veins on the ivy with green paste colour and alcohol.

Attach the dry lace pieces with royal icing, supporting them with sponge occasionally to lift them at an angle. Arrange them so that they are gradually lifting off the surface of the cake as a continuation of the stencil piece. Place a few flat onto the cakeboard itself as well.

9 To make the morning glory, colour some flower paste pink with a little red paste colour, take a small piece and roll it into a ball shape. Place it in the palm of your hand and roll one end to form a cone shape. Insert a cocktail stick into the wider end and gently roll backwards and forwards around the edge. Thin the edges as much as possible and curl them back a little. Make a variety of sizes, and a few buds, as well.

Secure a few small short stamens in the centre of the flowers with egg white, and leave to dry on a sponge. Dust the flowers with a touch of pink (red dusting colour and cornflour) around the edges and with a little green in the centre.

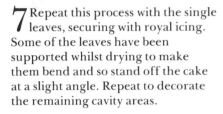

Creeping ivy and lace wedding cake

To complete the cake, simply secure the larger flowers into the cavities and the smaller among the ivy leaves with a little royal icing.

83

Cake for a Parachuting Enthusiast

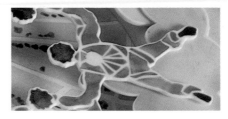

This cake is a very good example of how the stencilling technique is so adaptable. The overlapping stencils have been built up to create extra three-dimensional depth to add to that of the cavity feature. The strong, prominent shapes of clouds provide a simple but effective background.

The theme of parachuting is, I feel, a very diffi-cult one to portray successfully. There is always the desire to have the subjects almost floating above, somehow detached but not! My husband and his team recently represented Great Britain in the World Parachuting Championships in Thailand. As a gesture of good luck I made this cake to send them on their way.

REQUIREMENTS:

1 round cake, 25 cm (10″)
1 round cakeboard, 30 cm (12″)
900 g (2 lb) marzipan
900 g (2 lb) rolled fondant
    (sugarpaste)
350–450 g (¾–1 lb) mexican paste
royal icing
dusting colours: red, blue, black
    and green
cornflour (cornstarch)
jam

DECORATING TIME:
3–4 days

1 Once the cake has been cooked and cooled it has to be cut. Stand the cake on a work surface and mark a line 2.5 cm from the bottom all the way round. Using a very sharp knife (an electric knife is ideal), cut off this section following the guidelines. Remove this slice and cut a further circle out of its centre, approximately 15 cm (6″) in diameter.

2 Take away the centre piece and replace the remaining ring section onto the cake, securing with a thin layer of jam. Then marzipan the cake and leave to dry.

Mix up pale blue fondant, cover the cakeboard and dry overnight. With the remaining fondant, cover the cake and place onto the prepared board, smoothing out any indentations.

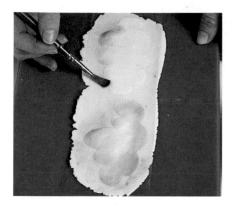

3 Make up the acetate stencils in the usual way (see page 9). Be prepared to allow at least 2 hours, as the freefall parachutists are particularly fiddly to do. Roll out the mexican paste and prepare the stencils for dusting as described on page 10.

Colour the parachutists first: dust up all the red areas with a reasonably small brush, followed by the blue and finally the black. Remove the excess dust with a puffer and peel off the acetate. Cut out the figures, leaving the central area to cut out last so that you can lean on it while cutting – it is important to avoid smudging the surface of the stencil.

Repeat this complex process when making clouds, varying the shades of grey with dusting. This can be done by adding a little cornflour to the dusting powder. Dry everything for at least 2 days.

4 Stencil the aerial view in the same way, using green dusting colour, but place it onto the centre of the cake as soon as it is ready. Leaving it to dry may mean forcing it into the middle, which could break it if it is a slightly tight fit. Paint on the tree details in dark green, and allow to dry.

5 Place 5 clouds evenly around the edge of the cake top, piping across their backs to secure them onto the cake. Leave to dry thoroughly. Attach the remaining clouds in the same way, supporting them with sponge once positioned to create a tiered effect.

6 The freefall parachutists can finally be secured onto the very top layer, giving them plenty of support underneath whilst drying.

7 Trace the outline of the small parachutists onto the sides of the cake. This is done by scratching with a pin through a traced drawing onto the icing. Then, using a no.00 tube, pipe over with white royal icing. (If you feel confident enough, you could pipe them on directly freehand, following a drawing as a guide.)

Pipe a scalloped edge around the base of the cake and cakeboard to complete the decoration of this stunning and unusual creation.

USEFUL SUPPLIERS AND ADDRESSES

The British Sugarcraft Guild
Wellington House, Messeter Place, Eltham, London SE9 5DP. 081 859 6943

The House of Sugarcraft
Suppliers of flower cutters, powder and paste colours and piping tubes. Unit 10, Broxhead Industrial Estate, Lindford Road, Bordon, Hampshire GU35 0NY

Cake Art Ltd
Wholesale suppliers of icings and equipment. Unit 16, Crown Close, Crown Industrial Estate, Priors Wood, Taunton;, Somerset TA2 8RX.

Sugarcraft Supplies PME (Harrow) Ltd
Suppliers of decorating equipment. Brember Road, South Harrow, Middlesex HA2 8UN.

Hammilworth Floral Products Ltd
Suppliers of stamens, wires, posy frills and ribbons. 23 Lime Road, Dumbarton, Dumbartonshire, Scotland G82 2RP.

JF Renshaw Ltd
Suppliers of icings. Locks Lane, Mitcham, Surrey CR4 2XG.

Cel Cakes
Suppliers of modelling tools, containers and display cabinets. Springfield House, Gate Helmsley, York, N. Yorkshire YO4 1NF.

Jenny Campbell Trading/BR Matthews and Son
12 Gypsy Hill, Upper Norwood, London SE19 1NN.

Mary Ford Cake Artistry Centre Ltd
28–30 Southbourne Grove, Southbourne, Bournemouth, Dorset BH6 3RA.

Woodnutts Ltd
97 Church Road, Hove, Sussex BN3 2BA.

A.O.K. Metals
16 Queensland Road, Bournemouth, BH5 2AB.

Essex Icing Centre
20 Western Road, Billericay, Essex CM12 9DZ.

British Bakels Ltd
238 Bath Road, Slough, SL1 4DU.

Sarah Waterkeyn
29 Lambs Conduit St, London, WC1N 3NG.

Sugarworks
161 Lower High Street, Stourbridge, West Midlands, DY8 1TS.

Cynthia Venn
3 Anker Lane, Stubbington, Fareham Hants PO14 3HF.

Knightsbridge Business Centre (Wilton UK)
Knightsbridge, Cheltenham, Gloucestershire, GL51 9TA.

Squires Kitchen
Squires House, 3 Waverley Lane, Farnham, Surrey, GU9 8BB.

Rainbow Ribbons
Unit D5, Romford Seedbed Centre, Davidson Way, Romford, Essex RM7 0AZ

House of Cakes
18 Meadow Close, Woodley, Stockport, Cheshire, SK6 1QZ.

MF Frames Ltd
10 St Helens Street, Ipswich, Suffolk, IP4 1HJ

UDO Ipswich
57/59 Upper Orwell Street, Ipswich, Suffolk

North America

ICES (International Cake Exploration Societe)
membership enquiries:
3087–30th St. S.W., Ste.101, Grandville, MI 49418.

maid of Scandinavia
(equipment, supplies, courses, magazine *Mailbox News*)
3244 Raleigh Avenue, Minneapolis, MN 55416.

Wilton Enterprises Inc
2240 West 75th Street, Woodridge, Illinois 60517.

Home Cake Artistry Inc
1002 North Central, Suite 511, Richardson, Texas 75080.

Lorraine's Inc
148 Broadway, Hanover, MA 02339.

Creative Tools Ltd
3 Tannery Court, Richmond Hill, Ontario, Canada, L4C 7V5.

McCall's School of Cake Decorating Inc
3810 Bloor Street West, Islington, Ontario, Canada, M9B 6C2.

Australia

Australian National Cake Decorators' Association
PO Box 321, Plympton, SA 5038.

Cake Decorating Association of Victoria
President, Shirley Vaas, 4 Northcote Road, Ocean Grove, Victoria 3226.

Cake Decorating Guild of New South Wales
President, Fay Gardiner, 4 Horsley Cres, Melba, Act,   2615.

Cake Decorating Association of Tasmania
Secretary, Jenny Davis, 29 Honolulu Street, Midway Point, Tasmania 7171.

Cake Decorators' Association of South Australia
Secretary, Lorraine Joliffe, Pindari, 12 Sussex Crescent, Morphet Vale, SA 5162.

Fer Lewis, Cake Ornament Company
156 Alfred Street, Fortitude Valley, Brisbane 4006.

Cake Ornament Co
156 Alfred Street, Fortitude Valley, Brisbane 4006.

New Zealand

New Zealand Cake Decorators Guild
Secretary, Morag Scott, 17 Ranui Terrace, Tawa, Wellington.

Decor Cakes
RSA Arcade, 435 Great South Road, Otahaha.

South Africa

South African Sugarcraft Guild
National Office, 1 Tuzla Mews, 187 Smit Street, Fairlan 2195.

Jem Cutters
PO Box 115, Kloof, 3 Nisbett Road, Pinetown 3600, South Africa.

INDEX